Dealing with Challenges

Grief and Loss

By Meg Gaertner

level
2
little blue
readers

www.littlebluehousebooks.com

Little Blue House is distributed by North Star Editions:
sales@northstareditions.com | 888-417-0195

Produced for Little Blue House by Red Line Editorial.

Photographs ©: Shutterstock Images, cover, 4, 7 (bottom), 8–9, 11 (top), 11 (bottom), 12 (top), 14–15, 18–19, 21 (top), 22–23, 24 (top right), 24 (bottom left), 24 (bottom right); iStockphoto, 7 (top), 12 (bottom), 16, 21 (bottom), 24 (top left)

Library of Congress Control Number: 2021916790

ISBN
978-1-64619-485-8 (hardcover)
978-1-64619-512-1 (paperback)
978-1-64619-564-0 (ebook pdf)
978-1-64619-539-8 (hosted ebook)

Printed in the United States of America
Mankato, MN
012022

About the Author

Meg Gaertner enjoys reading, writing, dancing, and being outside. She lives in Minnesota.

Table of Contents

Grief and Loss

People feel grief when they are dealing with loss.

Something important is gone.

They cannot get it back.

A loved one's death can cause grief.

A boy misses his grandfather.

He wishes his grandfather was still alive.

Moving to a new place can cause grief.

A girl misses her old house.

She wishes she still lived there.

Parents living apart can cause grief.

A boy misses spending time with both parents.

He wishes his parents still lived together.

parents

crying

yelling

Mixed Feelings

Grief shows up in many ways.

Some people feel very sad and cry.

Some people feel very angry and yell.

These feelings can come suddenly and change quickly.

Some people don't feel anything at all.

They sense a big hole in their lives, and they don't know how to fill it.

All of these feelings are okay.

Getting Help

Maybe you are feeling grief.

It can help to talk to someone.

Share your feelings with someone you love.

Maybe you aren't ready to talk.

Or maybe you don't know what to say.

That's okay, but don't hold your feelings inside.

Instead, draw a picture.

You could even dance to music.

These are some ways of letting

your feelings out.

Look at old photos, and remember happy times. You will always have these memories. You will make new happy memories, too.

photo

Glossary

grandfather

photo

house

picture

Index